Published 2008 by Concordia Publishing House
3558 S. Jefferson Avenue, St. Louis, MO 63118-3968
1-800-325-3040 • www.cph.org

Text © 2008 Dandi Daley Mackall
Illustrations © 2008 by Concordia Publishing House

Manufactured in China.

1  2  3  4  5  6  7  8  9  10        17  16  15  14  13  12  11  10  09  08

# the WonDer of Christmas

Written by Dandi Daley Mackall

Illustrated by Dave Hill

CONCORDIA PUBLISHING HOUSE • SAINT LOUIS

I wonder what the angels thought
When Almighty God said,
"The time is now!
I will send My Son."
Then He told them how.
Did the angels kneel
    in a giant bow?

I wonder what the angels thought.

I wonder, how did Gabriel feel

When he flew through time and through history
To a virgin girl down in Galilee,
And he brought Good News that would set us free.

I wonder, how did Gabriel feel?

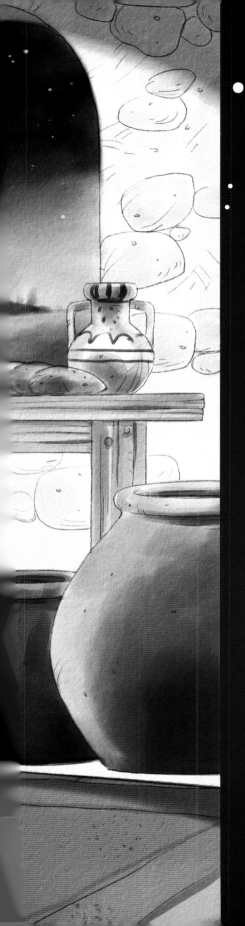

I wonder, what did Mary think

When she heard the news about God's own Son?
Could she be the mother of this chosen One?
When she bowed and said, "May Thy will be done,"

I wonder, what did
Mary think?

# I wonder, how did Joseph feel

When he heard the news and the gossip flew?
She'd be sent away—nothing else to do.
Then he learned the truth in a dream come true.

# I wonder, how did Joseph feel?

I wonder what the couple said
Down in Bethlehem, where the tax was paid.
Mary came along, though she might have stayed.
As the time drew near, and they talked and prayed,

I wonder what
          the couple said.

I wonder what the innkeeper thought
When he said,
"No room! Not here! No way!"
Did he change his mind when he let them stay
In the cold, dark barn on a bed of hay?

I wonder what
the innkeeper thought.

# I wonder how the shepherds felt.

When the angels came, shepherds bowed in fright.
Then they heard the news: "Christ is born this night!"
As they raced to see the amazing sight,

I wonder how the shepherds felt.

# I wonder what the Wise Men thought

As they rode, rode, rode,

Bearing gifts so far.

There was frankincense in a fancy jar.

As they kept their gaze on the brightest star,

# I wonder what the Wise Men thought.

# I wonder how I'll feel this year.

I will join the angels in a giant bow.
And I'll shout like Gabriel that the time is now.

# I will kneel like Mary,
# let my heart obey,

Maybe dream like Joseph when it's Christmas Day.

# I will run to Jesus
like the shepherds ran.

Like the Wise Men, I shall seek the Son of Man.

I'll be full of wonder as my Christmas starts,

And I'll think of Jesus in my heart of hearts.